Alonzo Ames Miner

The Rectitude of Government the Source of its Power

An Election Sermon

Alonzo Ames Miner

The Rectitude of Government the Source of its Power
An Election Sermon

ISBN/EAN: 9783337030889

Printed in Europe, USA, Canada, Australia, Japan

Cover: Foto ©Lupo / pixelio.de

More available books at **www.hansebooks.com**

The Rectitude of Government the Source of its Power.

AN

ELECTION SERMON

DELIVERED BEFORE

HIS EXCELLENCY BENJAMIN F. BUTLER,

GOVERNOR;

HIS HONOR OLIVER AMES,

LIEUTENANT-GOVERNOR;

THE HONORABLE COUNCIL, AND THE LEGISLA-
TURE OF MASSACHUSETTS,

IN

COLUMBUS AVENUE UNIVERSALIST CHURCH,

JANUARY 2, 1884,

BY

A. A. MINER, S.T.D., LL.D.,

BOSTON, PASTOR OF THE CHURCH.

BOSTON:
WRIGHT & POTTER PRINTING CO., STATE PRINTERS,
18 POST OFFICE SQUARE.
1884.

Commonwealth of Massachusetts.

BOSTON, JANUARY 16, 1884.

Rev. Dr. ALONZO A. MINER, Boston.

DEAR SIR: — I am directed by the Committee on Printing to invite you to furnish a copy of the "Annual Election Sermon," delivered by you on January 2d instant, to the end that it may be printed, as provided by the statutes.

I am,

Very respectfully, yours,

HOWES NORRIS,

Chairman of Committee on Printing.

BOSTON, JANUARY 18, 1884.

Hon. HOWES NORRIS.

DEAR SIR: — Herewith I transmit the manuscript of my Election Sermon, in accordance with your request.

Respectfully yours,

A. A. MINER.

The Rectitude of Government the Source of its Power.

PRELIMINARY ADDRESS.

Gentlemen of the Great and General Court:

Assembled here at the altar of God in the opening hour of your important duties, you will permit an humble citizen to congratulate you, who but yesterday stood among your fellow-citizens, upon the vast prerogatives committed to your hands. In the on-flowing of the stream of time, by the voice of this people, God has called you to be the government of Massachusetts for 1884. In some respects the most advanced Commonwealth in the entire galaxy of states, Massachusetts properly calls upon her most distinguished citizens to administer her affairs. It is a proud privilege, on general grounds, to be commissioned to preside over her varied interests, to conserve her good name in all things in which she merits it, and by a course of unquestionable patriotism win for her honors in fields she either has not entered, or has but timidly explored.

As the government of 1884, you can neither claim the honors already achieved, nor be held responsible for the stains upon her escutcheon that still remain. If you have come to your high duties with truly patriotic purpose, as we trust you have, unpledged to aught that can clip your wings in your flight toward the sun, you have opportunity for great service that should fill your hearts with inexpressible joy.

It cannot but be profitable, then, to spend here a brief hour in which may be struck the key-note of all divine harmonies in life, in duty, in destiny.

SERMON.

" JUSTICE AND JUDGMENT ARE THE HABITATION OF THY THRONE :
MERCY AND TRUTH SHALL GO BEFORE THY FACE."

Psalm lxxxix, 14.

Government is essentially a thing of principles.
All that is visible about a government is but its
machinery. Its offices, its elections, its function-
aries of various grades and duties, are transient
and changeable. The essential government, however, remains the same through all change.. This
essential element, invisible and abiding, is moral;
it is the element of rectitude, of truth and justice.
Penalties, however necessary and however faith-
fully inflicted, though a part of the machinery of
government, are more especially an indication of
the extent to which what is vital in the government has failed.

In the best governed home the machinery of
government has disappeared. The will of the
parent finds a welcome in the heart of the child.

That will is wisdom which the child has learned to appreciate and love. Penalty is not thought of; truth and duty fill the horizon, and peace blesses the home.

Perhaps our educational institutions make the nearest approach to this of any department of our government. Their strength lies in the natural justice they embody, the lack of which vitiates all governments. The distinguished Cudworth says: "Covenants without natural justice are nothing but mere words and breath, and therefore can have no force to oblige. * * * None can be obliged in duty to obey, but by natural justice. * * * Whatever is iniquitous can never be made lawful by any power on earth."

GOVERNMENT THE HIGHEST FUNCTION OF MAN.

Substantially moral, government thus becomes the highest and divinest function of man — the embodiment of justice and truth. Recognizing the vital relations of the whole people, it aims to give protection to every genuine interest. Its pathway lies above the plane of passion, appetite, greed, unholy competitions, and every form of sinister ambition and self-seeking. It stretches out ts arms to raise up the fallen; never to cast down others among them. Its power dwells in its righteousness. Truth is at once its life-blood, its weapon of aggressiveness, and its assured defence. It is this invisible power that makes Christ a king. He says: "My kingdom is not of this world: if my kingdom were of this world, then would my servants fight, that I should not be delivered to the Jews." He was delivered, condemned, crucified. All power seemed against him; in fact, all power was with him. What was meant to be, and seemed, his utter overthrow, was but the foundation of a triumph that has enthroned his name above every name. What is power in Christ's kingdom would be power in all kingdoms.

Human law is nothing of itself. Its majesty and strength are borrowed. Cicero says: "Law is right reason, congruous to nature, pervading all minds, constant, eternal, which calls to duty by its commands, and repels from wrongdoing by its prohibitions. * * * This law cannot be annulled, superseded, or over-ruled. No senate, no people can loose us from it; no interpreter can explain it away. It is not one law at Rome, another at

Athens; one at present, another at some future time; but one law, perpetual and immutable, includes all nations and all times. Of this law, the author and giver is God." Milton says, any statute "repugnant to the will of God and to right reason is null and void." St. Augustine declares that, "in temporal laws nothing is righteous or lawful, but what the people have derived to themselves out of the Law Eternal."

Even the divine government stands by its rectitude. God's throne — the symbol of his power — dwells in justice and judgment. These are its habitation; while mercy and truth illumine his pathway. Could righteousness and truth forsake his throne, his government would be government no longer. Chaos would reign and all forces become lawless. A wild railway train, rushing on in its mad career, with no engineer's hand to guide it, freighted with hundreds of precious lives and untold commercial wealth, spreading destruction on either hand, until hurled into some yawning gulf in irremediable ruin — would be but a faint illustration of the devastation and woe that would attend the forces of nature when no longer dominated by intelligence and righteousness.

If this would be true of the divine government, how much more of human governments. Over against the lawlessness of natural forces would stand the vagrant ambitions of all who have any part in the functions of government. The visible processes, the ostensible aims, the cunning manipulation of those functions, would still go on; but all that constitutes these functions a government would have departed, leaving a semblance of government operated by a chaos of passions to selfish ends.

ROOTS OF GOVERNMENT.

The roots of government are not arbitrary assumptions. They involve certain absolute and universal principles — principles which fasten upon every man, woman and child; involve their relationship to each other and to the government itself; make the welfare of each the welfare of all, and the defection of each the curse of all — principles out of which, as the French phrase it, springs the solidarity, not of a city, state, or nation alone, but of the whole human race — which must be recognized and acted upon to secure the highest good of any, and the disregard of which blasts the

hopes of all. Such disregard not only voids the
moral power of a government, but blackens it with
rapacity and usurpation.

Hence the very beginnings of ostensible government go far to determine its character. Citizens, more or less numerous, organize for
political ends, — presumably for patriotic ends, —
presumably to grapple with and sternly remove
any great evil under which the commonwealth
suffers. To reject such work is to emasculate
the movement at the outset, and make themselves
cumberers of the ground. Manifold social dangers
are to be guarded against. The ignorant must be
enlightened, the poor fed, causes of disease removed, robbers guarded against, passion controlled,
criminal enterprises suppressed, public indecencies
prevented, free commerce in all things useful en-
couraged, sympathetic relations between employers
and employees fostered, liberal expenditures in
support of educational and other beneficent institutions and economy in all else practised, inex-
pensive and prompt execution of the laws guaran-
teed, and the general welfare promoted. As said
an English statesman, "it is the very business of
government to make it as easy as possible to do

right, and as difficult as possible to do wrong." Presumably this is what any conspicuous political movement means.

THE TEMPTATION.

But, adopting the aphorism of the old Syrian philosopher: "To-day ought to be the disciple of yesterday," how almost instinctively do we assume degeneracy from our ideal. Not only do we come short of these high ends, but often turn our backs upon them, and not seldom deliberately strengthen the evils we should remove.

Let us consider the marvellous course of this degeneracy.

Its source, I need not say, is in the vitiated state of the public mind. The public thought is modified by numerous collateral influences. The press profits by conforming to it, and in turn often intensifies and emboldens what is evil in it. Aspirants for place are careful not to rebuke it, if they do not apologize for or even defend it. The clergy become discreet in view of it, and deal in "glittering generalities." Severe in their forms of faith, they kindly point sinners-in-the-abstract to the warm welcome they will receive beyond the Styx; but the only *infernum* they appear to believe in for clerical sinners-in-the-concrete, who rashly reject campaign dicta, is the hell of current unpopularity.

By a kind of physiological law, this poison in the body politic, like a cancer in the human body, sends its death-dealing influence through all its veins and arteries, undermining its constitution, wasting its substance, and gravely threatening its entire overthrow.

The diagnosis of the disease is not difficult. What the more clamorous and less scrupulous of the voting population desire is carefully noted. A committee, not wholly self-constituted, whose topmost aim is success at whatever cost, survey the field; put out feelers through the press, watching the responses; gradually concentrate public attention upon some one man or measure, and thus create a boom that shall enable them to rouse the public heart.

Then comes a convention. The genius of the committee displays itself; for, be it remembered, the committee is the convention ; and the convention is the committee inflated. Trained in its duties, it returns a clean-cut echo to every note the committee sounds in its ears.

Next, its platform — what shall it be? Measures involving the highest good of the state? That would be the course of patriots ; and however small the number ready to sustain such measures, they would be emphasized and insisted on. The campaign would then be a great missionary struggle in which mercy and truth would emblazon the banner, and justice and judgment sound the bugle call to duty.

But this convention is organizing for numerical success. Measures involving the highest good of the state would alienate all its criminal classes. Numerical success without them is impossible. We cannot wait for the slow process of lifting them up to us ; we must therefore go down to them. True, they are the dregs of the city, but they are the make-weight in its overshadowing influence. We cannot offend them and win. We must divide them and secure a portion at least of this despicable following to swell our retinue and illumine the glory of our victory.

Conforming to these exigencies, our committee avoid as much as possible what is vital in the inter-

ests of the hour, applaud the achievements of the
more or less distant past, pour broadsides of hot
shot — oftentimes of personal and party malignity,
under the thin guise of righteous indignation —
into the ranks of their hereditary foe, and then call
loudly upon the entire commonwealth to mark the
splendors of their achievements.

As accidents are liable to happen, however, and
as resolutions may be thrust in demanding an in-
convenient expression where it was predetermined
to be silent, a pit for such missiles is commonly dug
by referring all resolutions to a committee who will
judiciously forget to report on them. Not a word
is permitted to be uttered save by the trusted servants of the proposed method of success. The
nominations are made, the nominees commonly
handicapped, and the campaign begins.

Where now is the moral power of such a convention? Not in its high moral aims ; it repudiated
these in the beginning. Not in the tone of its
following ; it deliberately lowered that tone for
numbers. Not in its nominees, however excellent
in personal character ; for they represent not themselves, but the emptiness of their platform. Not
only is its moral power gone, but a kind of neces-

sity, springing from its environment, compels all who follow its lead to do mischief throughout the struggle. Though themselves silent on highest matters, there are others who will not be silent. To counteract their influence and secure the necessary numbers, highest matters must be depreciated or perverted, and the judgment of citizens corrupted, until honest men, both clerical and lay, are seduced to the support of measures they loathe.

THE CORRUPTION SPREADS.

This viciousness of the beginnings tends to corruption in all subsequent stages. The divine prerogatives of the franchise are employed to personal ends. Legislation is shaped, not by the evils to be removed, but by the perpetrators of those evils who resist their removal. Innumerable apologies for the wrongs thus committed are made to solace troubled consciences, and the rougher work is passed over to the less scrupulous co-operators. Innocent maxims misapplied, blind the eye, deafen the ear, and harden the heart. The " half-loaf" adage is made to justify compromises that surrender the field to evil. The duty of "taking the world as one finds it," is made an excuse for leav-

ing it in the same condition, or even in a worse
one. Voting for righteousness in a minority, is
assumed to be " the throwing away of one's vote ;"
while the truth is the compromising of one's conscience, with however great a majority, is the
throwing away of the voter.

BRIBERY.

Undoubtedly the corruption of the ballot, politi-
cally speaking, is the giant evil of our land. We
carefully guard by penalties against bribery by
money ; but are there no briberies by office, by indirect and incidental gains, by the profits of criminal business, by the promise of legislation for pet
measures? Constituted as our government is, are
not the very evils, which make government necessary, bribes to the nullifying of its power?

It is stated that at our recent city election, voters
in a state of helpless inebriety had ballots thrust
into their hands, and were lifted by fellow-voters
to the ballot-box, to express their patriotic judgment in favor of license.

But acting with others, it is said, is a necessity
under popular governments ; and if we refuse co-
operation because of the support we should give to

criminal enterprises, others will combine to give us
a still worse government. It is a matter of grave
doubt when we have brought ourselves to vote for
cr'minal measures, whether there is any danger of
others doing worse. Should they attempt it, however, they would have our example for a defence.
The highest moral service a man can render is not
unfrequently to step squarely out and refuse all
participation in current evils. Sinning is not at all
a question of garb. The highest and the lowest
ranks of society meet together. The one, it may
be, in broadcloth ; the other in rags ; but they
drink the same beer. There they are on a level.
Disgraceful, shameful, but true!

SANCTION NULLIFIES LIMITATION.

Our theory of sanctioning an evil that we may
limit it, is but a dream. Those who ask for such
laws want the sanction but by no means the limitations. In practice they always resist, and suc-
cessfully resist the limitations whatever they may
be. The vaunted restrictions which we put into
law, are not, never were, never will be, were never
intended to be, and never can be executed. For
ten days in November 1872, independent of all

law, the dram-shop business in Boston was closed by the chief of police; besides which period, there probably has not been one hour, night or day, Sundays included, for fifty years, when a citizen could not somewhere get his dram. In giving our sanction to such evils, we cast away all moral power. Our sanction repudiates the divine law. The violator of our restrictions tramples only on human law, and places himself on our broader repudiation. He stands with us on the same base of evil.

OFFICERS, NOT CITIZENS, EXECUTORS OF LAW.

The acknowledged weakness of existing criminal laws is sometimes urged as a ground of their continuance, — the specious plea being, "We have more law than the people will execute." The truth is, we have laws that cannot be executed — laws that would not cure the evils ostensibly aimed at, if they were executed. We refuse to enact laws that can be executed, and which if executed would be a remedy, — refuse. because they can be executed, and because if executed they would be a remedy.

But the plea is radically objectionable in another

particular. It assumes that the people, in their capacity as citizens, should execute the laws; while, in fact, having determined by law what should be done, they provide themselves with officers of the law to do it, and tax themselves liberally to pay them.

Here the State is doomed to still further disappointment. The moment those officers of the law meet with difficulty, which will be the moment they enter honestly upon their duty, and find their nerve, integrity and manliness subjected to fearful strain, they turn pale, desert their post, and claim that public opinion does not sustain them. They do not resign, throw up the emoluments of office, and take themselves out of the way — which would be decent and manly; but continue nominally the servants of the state, accept the bribes of inefficiency, and nullify the law — which is indecent, unmanly.

The only public opinion an officer of the law has a right to know anything about is that which has been expressed through the forms of law. Any other yielding to a supposed public opinion subjects us to a government of men who arbitrarily displace the government of laws. Thus in casting

aside patriotic integrity and high moral obligation
at the outset, we lay the foundation for, and by
our example justify, the vitiating of governmental
processes at every stage.

All too emphatic an illustration of these principles is furnished in the history of our own Commonwealth. From 1855 to 1868, a law stood
graven on our statute-books, luminous in its
righteousness; constitutionally unassailable; before
which the government of the Commonwealth trem-
bled like an aspen leaf for twelve long years, lacking
equally the courage to repeal it and the manliness to
execute it; in whose iron grip the stoutest violators
were dashed to the earth, — six hundred of whom
in the space of four weeks, in 1867, pledged themselves to the district attorney of Suffolk County that
if the State was in earnest they would not contend,
but would surrender the business; a law which
withstood like an adamantine wall the shocks of
its violators; and against which the syren influence
of a martialed array of ex-officials, dignitaries,
clergy, physicians and citizens, vainly led by the
most distinguished ex-governor Massachusetts

ever had, under the specious pretext of substituting for it something more efficient — in connection with his colleague exhibiting an ability and energy for which its violators gladly paid $15,000 to the one and $5,000 to the other, — all in the name of the merchants of Boston, while both they and the merchants were the tools of men whom the law would have sent to prison — such a law, impregnable by open assault, yielded at length to covert foes attacking it through "ways that were dark, and tricks that were vain."

A single year, however, of the unmitigated woes that followed, produced on the part of the State a spontaneous purpose, as evinced in the election, to return to the law which had been lost.

OFFICIAL WEAKNESS.

Notwithstanding this decided action of the Commonwealth in the proposed restoration of the law — action which should have emboldened the timid, removed all mental confusion, and strengthened the feeble knees — its good work was nullified by the weakness of a governor, who, counselled by men, partisans first and patriots afterwards, broke the integrity of the law, and opened the way for its complete destruction. By this rupture, seemingly of slight importance, as by the puncture of an artery in the human body, all its life-blood soon ran out.

Fifteen years have elapsed, and the policy of the state, by insensible stages, has been entirely reversed. Suppression has given place to protection. Partisan policy has triumphed over righteous principle; and the moral confidence of the people is paralyzed.

When will a change come? It is said, "Public opinion is not yet ripe for it." It was ripe fifteen years ago; why is it corrupt to-day? What is the government doing to ripen it and restore the moral tone of the past? By what philosophy do we expect to raise up public opinion, while we are steadily dragging it down? How long will it take three hundred thousand determined supporters of an evil to accomplish the suppression of that evil?

DIFFERENCES OF OPINION.

But it is claimed that there are differences of opinion about the evils themselves. I deny it — deliberately, emphatically, solemnly deny it. King and clown, barrister and blackleg, grocer and

groom, clergy and laity, cooper and carpenter, phy-
sician and fool, all alike know that these evils are
simply indescribable. The arguments of the ab-
stainer and the excuses of the drinker, the pleader
for suppression and the struggler for toleration,
alike show that these woes are known and read of
all men. There are, indeed, alleged differences o
opinion, growing out of real differences of temptation, in view of which angels weep and broken-
hearted mothers die.

It was the same when the curse of slavery was
upon us. A few men and women made themselves
heard, as with the voice of the clarion, through all
the land. The cry of fanaticism was raised against
them from one end of the country to the other, and
a price was set upon their heads. Meantime fugi-
tive slaves were hunted like wild beasts. Nobody
remembered that the black man is a brother. The
South professed to believe that slavery was a great
missionary institution for the salvation of the black
race. The North doubted its original divinity, but
because of the compromises of our fathers believed
it a duty to maintain it.

We found ourselves slave-catchers, indeed, but
it brought us special political and commercial ad-

vantages. Even our clergy rose to the dignity of defending slavery from the Bible — adducing Paul's letter to Philemon to whom he sent back the bond-servant Onesimus — forgetting, however, Paul's special charge to Philemon, to receive Onesimus as no longer a bond-servant, but as a brother beloved. Now that slavery is removed, not only is the judgment of politicians corrected, but there is scarcely a belated priest in all the pulpits of Christendom that dreams of defending it. The simple solution is, temptation is gone.

So when our descendants shall have escaped from the chronic curse of Christendom, they will look back with unutterable shame upon their lineage. They can then estimate the quality of our intelligence, the shocking immorality of our ethics, the stupidity of our economics, and the hollowness of our religion, in which we celebrate the death of our Lord in a wine as spurious as our patriotism and as hypocritical as our piety.

UNANIMITY IN METHOD.

Nor are there, among earnest people, any grave differences in respect to methods of dealing with our overshadowing woes. A timid, half-hearted, meddling policy has prevailed for centuries. This has worn out the patience of the public, aroused the anger of the vicious, and left the evil to develop itself in its own destructive way. Those wishing to put an end to these woes are substantially agreed in regard to method. With wondrous unanimity, through all sections of our country, and on both sides of the Atlantic, these demand unqualified suppression.

Those who seek only limitation of the evils, keeping an open door for personal indulgence, talk wisely about " regulation."   And, in their pretended desire to " regulate," they make about every ten years the circuit of all possible shifts in the law — from screen to back-door and back-door to screen, from Sundays to midnight and midnight to Sundays, from minors to drunkards and drunkards to minors, from landlords to tenants and tenants to landlords, taking in school-house and civil-damage laws by the way — like the goose that stands on one leg till weary, then shifts to the other — remaining a goose, however, all the same.

Of the 125 men called, in 1867, to testify before a joint committee of the legislature in favor of " regulation " as against prohibition, but a single one of the number denied that he was a patron of the cup. Such men keep an eye to their own convenience, and cannot be expected to give a verdict against themselves.

Under the existing state of our laws, the moral power of the best sentiment of the Commonwealth is weakened, and the practical result of its expression in a large measure lost. The great majority of the towns and many of the cities vote to suppress the traffic ; but their proximity to other towns and cities voting adversely, deprives them of a large measure of the advantages they would otherwise enjoy, both in regard to excluding the prohibited commodity and paralyzing the arm of the civil authorities in executing the law.

Besides, the Commonwealth is disintegrated. The cities and towns voting for suppression, abandon the sober, industrious, prudent citizens of other municipalities, and especially of Boston, to be the prey of the criminal depredators with which they abound. This abandonment of its best citizens on the part of the State, not to say its treachery towards them, cannot be too strongly condemned. Why should an honest man living in the neighborhood of thieves be subjected to the pleasure of those thieves whether to rob him or not.

DUTIES OF THE STATE.

The State has duties towards all its citizens — not simply to punish criminals after the act ; but as far as possible to prevent the crime itself. The State is the law-maker. Having enacted wholesome laws, it should have the manliness to see them executed. It is paltry to give a man the privilege of voting a nuisance next door to me, when he would not tolerate it next door to himself. It is paltry for the State to cast off its legislative responsibilities that it may have smoother sailing on the dead sea of politics. It is more than paltry — it is criminal in the State to expose the lives of wives and children to the fury of husbands and fathers sent home dehumanized from our thousands of "regulated" fountains of death. The wife is powerless ; the children are powerless ; the maddened husband is free till the terrible crime is committed. Then the royal dignity of the law steps in to punish. Whom? The criminal law-maker? The commissioner who so judiciously does the "regulating?" The servant of the State who deals

out the potations? None of these! The wretch
who was first tempted, then debauched, then infu-
riated, and finally ground to powder between the
upper and nether millstone of the " State-regu-
lated" machinery for supplying victims to the
courts, the prisons, and the gallows — he is the
culprit. Does punishing him bring back the wife
or children? Does it awake the State to a sense
of its diabolism? Does it disturb the pious devo-
tions of men who rent their real estate at a hundred
per cent advance for purposes of evil, and then pray
God to put an end to such evils? Moral power in
governments! — seemingly so deep is the abyss in
which they are sunk that plummet and line cannot
fathom it. Publius Syrus says, " The judge is condemned when the guilty is acquitted."

But all is not lost. There is a protesting sense
of responsibility in thousands of breasts which
calls a halt. Who can better afford to hear that
call than the legislature before me? Untrammelled,
I trust, by any embarrassing pledges ; free to
speak the best word and do the best thing with
boldness and emphasis ; you can strike the key-
note of measures that will crown the State with
honor.

ABANDON THE RUTS.

But you must escape from the ruts. You need not sound a trumpet before you. Your action, however, must be unambiguous and firm. Evil is far from being formidable when it is heroically confronted. The tiger quails when you look him sharply in the eye. Besides, unexpected allies will arise. Many a man is held in the ranks of the foe by the force of his surroundings. Such will welcome deliverance. Many a conscience, long repressed, is ready to assert itself and come to your aid. Many a citizen, apathetic through despair, will enter with a bound the resurrection life. Let your good work be pronounced, and the State will draw a deep breath of satisfaction.

First of all give over all thoughts of the people executing the laws. Bid the proper officers, whom the people have provided, execute them. If they fail, remove them. Look about yourselves, and you will find great resources at your command for such a work. If you do not find them, make them. A new life would thus be at once breathed into law ; and all around you the dead would live.

GOVERN THE CITIES.

Apply this thoroughness especially to cities. Reject absolutely the assumption that cities cannot be governed. The chronic method of shamming the government must be abolished. The discriminations unknown to the law must cease. There can be no government where the victim in broadcloth is sent by carriage to his home, and the victim in corduroys is sent by the court to Deer Island. Let law be alike law on Beacon Street and on North Street. A change of *personnel* in the officers may be necessary. Bouncing beer-barrels may be very inadequate protection against beershops. But Berkshire hills abound in living springs ; and the chief Executive possesses great, though hitherto unused, powers.

TRUST THE PEOPLE.

Then, by all means, trust the people. Trust them as a whole — not in detachments — not in squads — not in guerilla bands of covert marauders. Trust the rank and file of the great army of patriots on the open battle-field of the State. Fear not to submit to them the highest questions. Let them pronounce as a whole whether they will be governed from above or from beneath. There can be little doubt of their decision. The thirteen cities of the State, voting Dec. 4, taken together, declared themselves patriots. Boston, even, Dec. 11, suggests an interesting query. Casting over 53,000 votes for mayor, it gave less than 23,000 for license, and more than 13,000 against license ; while more than 17,000 voting for mayor did not vote on the dram-shop question.

Notice three things : 1. The friends of the dram-shop are, doubtless, mainly included in the 23,000 yea votes. 2. The majority of yeas over nays was less than 10,000 votes. 3. Had the 17,-000 non-voters, many of whom were apathetic because they deemed the effort useless, given their judgment at the polls, it is probable that the 10,000 license majority would have been overcome, and some thousands scored on the side of righteousness. However that may be, there is little doubt that any excess that might have remained, would be largely overborne by the decisive action of other parts of the State.

MAGNITUDE OF THE PROBLEM.

And what a problem is this! The *New York Tribune*, since the days of Horace Greeley never suspected of radicalism, under the title of " SIZE OF THE TEMPERANCE QUESTION," gave a long and serious editorial, Sept. 27, 1882, from which I make the following extracts:

" It does no good for men to sneer at the agitation in regard to the liquor traffic. The subject is too important to be laughed down."

*   *   *   *   *   *   *   *   *   *

" Aside from the law-defying spirit which it has elicited, aside from all its moral and religious aspects, the question considered purely as one of dollars and cents, in its effect upon the national prosperity and wealth, is one of the most important that can be named."

"Directly and indirectly, this country spends in the liquor traffic every year a sum exceeding half the national debt. The cost of that traffic to the country, direct and indirect, is greater than the profits of all its capital not invested in real estate. It costs every year more than our whole civil service, our army, our navy, our congress, including the river and harbor and the pension bills, our wasteful local governments, and all national, state, county and local debts, besides all the schools in the country. In fact, this nation pays more for liquor than for every function of every kind of government. How is a question of that size to be put aside with a sneer?"

*　*　*　*　*　*　*　*　*　*

" There is certainly spent for drink more than $800,-000,000, and the entire sum raised by taxes of all kinds, national, state, county, city, town and school district, is stated on authority of the Census Bureau to be not more than about $700,000,000."

" But the cost of the liquor drunk is not by any means the whole cost of the liquor traffic. An official report, prepared with much labor by the Bureau of Statistics of Massachusetts, under authority from the legislature, states that 84 per cent of all the crime and criminal expenses in that State comes directly from the abuse of liquor. There are at least one in twenty of the able-bodied men in this country who are rendered idle by their habits or incapacitated for work, and these persons, at the ordinary wages of working men, would earn, if industrious and fairly employed, over $200,000,000 yearly."

*　*　*　*　*　*　*　*　*　*

" But the time has gone by in this country when a serious discussion of a question that involves such a vast expense to the nation can be prevented by bullying, intolerance, insolence or ridicule. This very practical people, having begun to think about the matter in earnest, perceives that it is much too important to be put aside at the dictation of saloon-keepers. It is certain that the entire savings of the people and all additions to their wealth are not twice as much as the sum expended for

liquor, and because of the abuse of liquor. If any just
and reasonable proposition can be made that will add one-
half to the savings and the prosperity of the nation, it
will not be put down by a sneer, nor defeated by a law-
breaking mob."

Consider well these extracts. Why should the
enormous burden of the drink tax, $800,000,000 a
year, continue to rest upon our country; or $30,-
000,000 a year on our own Commonwealth? All
this, with a like sum to repair the damages, is an
utter and absolute waste; though some political
economists do not appear to know it. Gather the
cereals of a country, convert them into whiskey
or beer, transport it to tide-water, pour it into the
sea — is there any doubt that it would be an
utter and shameful waste? Is it any the less a
waste if on its way to the sea, in the language
of the eloquent Chapin, "it is strained through
the human stomach and spoils the strainer?"

HOLOCAUST OF A HUNDRED THOUSAND LIVES.

Out of the holocaust of a hundred thousand lives,
annually sacrificed in our country to Bacchus and
Gambrinus — *we are not heathens; we are a Chris-
tian people* — four thousand of them fill newly

made graves in Massachusetts soil. Thousands
more, enslaved by appetite, are in daily training to
follow in their turn. Monday morning, Dec. 17,
one hundred and five victims passed through the
Central Municipal Court of Boston alone, leaving
the South Boston, Charlestown and Highland
courts unreported. And this was by no means a
"field day." Meantime every hospital, inebriate
home and place of confinement is crowded with
fruits of the dram-shop.

This shocking sacrifice of life, it may be re-
marked, does not appear in our records. We tax
ourselves liberally to prepare elaborate tables
of registration, that the causes of disease and
death may be known and the general health promoted; and then falsify those records to keep
ourselves in countenance. In multitudes of in-
stances, congestion of the lungs, liver, stomach,
kidneys, and the like, is made the agent of death,
where undeniably whiskey strikes the fatal blow.
We have high authority for saying: "Evil men
and seducers wax worse and worse, deceiving and
being deceived."

PROHIBITORY AMENDMENT.

Let me, then, earnestly urge you, gentlemen, to submit to the whole people the question whether they will prohibit in the fundamental law of the State the further destruction of our citizens at the hands of the government. It is the people's question. They have a right to pronounce upon it. Let no man claim to be a patriot and withhold his voice from giving them the opportunity in this year of grace 1884. If in your minds there is any doubt of success, let a campaign be fought on that issue.

The State of Iowa should be your inspiration. One of the great parties of the State espoused the cause of good order, urged the constitutional amendment, press and platform taking up the battle-cry, and won a victory both for themselves and their cause.

Ohio, on the other hand, was halting, cautious, craven ; and, finally casting its fortunes into the scale of misrule, it lost — though the cause of reform itself came well-nigh succeeding ; perhaps by an honest count would have succeeded.

An Ohio correspondent, the Rev. E. A. Stone, of Galion, in *The Watchman* of this city, Dec. 27,

1883, makes the following very emphatic statements :

" The returns since the battle from all sections of the State show that had the votes been honestly counted, the amendment was carried by an overwhelming majority, and this is not guess-work, but careful counts and estimates from all sections. We have sat down supinely and submitted to the greatest disgrace that ever fell on a free people, the violent, wilful and deliberate setting aside of our united voice at the ballot-box. Shout it out to the whole land,— *Ohio carried the second amendment, but the leaders of both the great parties were so corrupted by the money power of the liquor traffic that they have refused to listen to the voice of the majority.* The conviction of every investigator must be that the majority for prohibition was large, in spite of the antagonism of every political paper of importance, and of the leading speakers and candidates of both parties. We were simply defrauded out of that which we won by the hardest of work and the honest purpose of our best citizens."

If such statements are true, pray how much of our boasted liberties remain to us? Is not the high moral vote of the North of as much consequence as the empty partisan vote of the South? May not the earnest temperance workers of Maryland, South Carolina, and Georgia fling back to the North the taunt : " Give us an honest count? "

The *Boston Daily Advertiser*, under date of Oct. 7, 1882, falls into the following inadvertence :

" The liquor dealers are forcing the issue here as they are in the Western States, and here, as there, the sober, industrious, intelligent and moral forces of the community will rally to the security of their interests with great disregard of political party ties.   Massachusetts does not, any more than does Ohio or Kansas or Maine, believe that the business which produces the larger part of all the misery, want and crime against which the State has to guard should go unregulated or be subject to inefficient regulation."

Does the *Advertiser* believe that the liquor traffic is " *efficiently regulated?* "   Hear it further :

" It may as well be understood that the alternative or such a statute as the State now has is not a less stringent, but a more stringent one."

Thus does that dignified defender of license confess we are not doing the best possible to restrain the abominations of the drink traffic, and warns the dealer that a more repressive law may be feared. Surely " confession is good for the soul."

Who doubts that a campaign on this issue, fought with anything like the energy that has marked the recent campaigns in our Commonwealth would be eminently successful? How almost infinitely does it transcend any issue recently before us. It is unworthy of Massachusetts to rise in mass against a single man, who has neither destroyed a life nor squandered a dollar, and leave this gigantic criminality to flaunt the black flag of death in our faces unchallenged and untouched. Let the meagreness of the majority in so tremendous a vote, warn us that there is a lack of fundamental satisfaction — not with candidates, but with issues.

OTHER DANGERS.

There are other evils flourishing on Massachusetts soil which should not be overlooked. In the aggregate, the woes they inflict are great. But when the drink curse shall have been removed, and the smoke and dust of the conflict shall have cleared away, the greater part of our remaining ills will have disappeared. With a clear eye, a level head, and a steady hand, we shall be able, by accurate, repeated, well-directed blows, to demolish the lesser of the outgrowths of evil springing from other roots.

There are dangers, however, of the most threatening proportions, quite too long neglected, and to

which both our civil authorities and the secular
and religious press pay altogether undue deference.
There are hundreds of thousands of persons annually coming to our shores, untrained in our indus-
tries, alien from our thought, and antagonistic to
our institutions. Many of these, as well as of
others native to the soil, are gathered into houses
secluded from the public, whose history and fortunes are never known. Their children by thousands are withdrawn from the public schools, left
to roam the streets, or placed in parochial schools,
under the specious plea of securing to them moral
and religious training, from entering which our
school authorities are debarred, leaving them to
the exclusive supervision and direction of the Rom-
ish priesthood. Here they are educated as a caste,
out of sympathy with us as a people, and the ready
tools of the most wily foe that has ever assailed the
liberties of the world.

It becomes a grave problem how a free country,
with popular institutions, tolerating all religions,
and respecting in all freedom of conscience, should
bear itself towards a confessed foe of its most vital
policy. It is a grave problem whether such a
country should harbor within its borders, institu-

tions she may not systematically visit and circumstantially inspect by proper officers at any time. It is an equally grave problem whether she should welcome to citizenship anybody acknowledging superior allegiance to any foreign potentate whatsoever. As foreigners and religionists, we welcome them, with all the world, as men and brethren; but as depredators upon human liberty, whether civil or religious, we reject them with the utmost intensity of purpose. *To tolerate intolerance is to convert our toleration into intolerance.* Conserve these principles, and we shall enjoy a higher and diviner civilization than the world has ever yet seen.

FUNDAMENTAL TRUTH.

In all our studies of the problems of social life, there is one fundamental truth which should be our constant inspiration: " God hath made of one blood all nations of men to dwell upon the face of all the earth." Every man is the brother of every other man. Not one of all these who fall out by the way, is alien from us. Of whatsoever land, race, or nationality, he is our brother. His interest is our interest — not constructively, or by the cant of pulpit or sect; but in deepest truth; in profoundest

reality. When he suffers, we suffer; when he is
blest, we are blest. In nature, in rights, in interest, in destiny, one. All substantial advancement
must take all men along.

We must beware, therefore, of cliques, and parties, and sectional interests that shall in anywise
bar our endeavors to promote the welfare of the
entire Commonwealth, and build her fortunes level
to the highest possibilities. God delights in the
good of all his children.

In closing, your Excellency will permit me to
proffer you respectful salutations. Your great success through a long professional career, achieved
by extraordinary ability and rare personal energy,
command in this hour of retirement from the gu-
bernatorial office general recognition. Your many
labors on more conspicuous theatres have become
matters of history. As our great internecine war
was coming on, you warned the South of the issue
of its madness. You counselled the North of its
threatening dangers, its necessity for preparation,
and the duty of decisive action — backing your
counsel by braving the dangers of the battle-field.
The nation was taught by you to regard the negro
as a " contraband of war." Your heroic rectitude

and firm justice in New Orleans made you conspicuous on both sides of the Atlantic. A similar heroism as Governor of Massachusetts, in the face of as bitter partisanship as often falls to the lot of a public man to encounter, cannot but be salutary in its influence upon all but weak men among your successors. The hearty good wishes of multitudes will follow you whithersoever you go.

And as I turn to your Honor the Lieutenant Governor, the honorable Council, and members of the Legislature, I beg to extend to you kindred congratulations. Many of you have rendered noble service in varied public positions. You must all be aware how evanescent and valueless are the honors of sinister service, no matter by what multitudes awarded. On the other hand, profound and abiding is the satisfaction of having contributed to build the state in righteousness, and promote the welfare of succeeding generations. Let a sacred ambition command your noblest service; and the plaudits of the Highest, waking echoes in the hearts of the lowliest, will crown your days with the " peace that passeth all understanding."